POWER YOUR CREATIVE BRAIN

Jan Parker

MEMORIES Write dreams

thoughts ideas

draw songs

Colour & Create

ART THERAPY - BASED EXERCISES

I

For Sian

First published January 2018

PARKER PUBLICATIONS

ART WORK Jan Parker

TECHNICAL EDITOR Matthew Fordham

ISBN 978-0-9957498-3-2

4

Your poems + songs

CARNIVAL

feelings

Fashion

memories

Your drawings + ideas

Poster

NATURE'S KNOTS

NATURE'S KNOTS

fashion

hobbies

Your thoughts + notes

dreams

Your poems + songs

Advert

thoughts + notes

Memories

Your drawings + ideas

BIRTHDAY WISHES

songs

ZODIAC

drawings + ideas

ZODIAC

Memories

AiR

book cover

Your thoughts + notes

SIGNS

games

fashion

FILMS

Your thoughts + notes

Your drawings + ideas

Poster

Advert

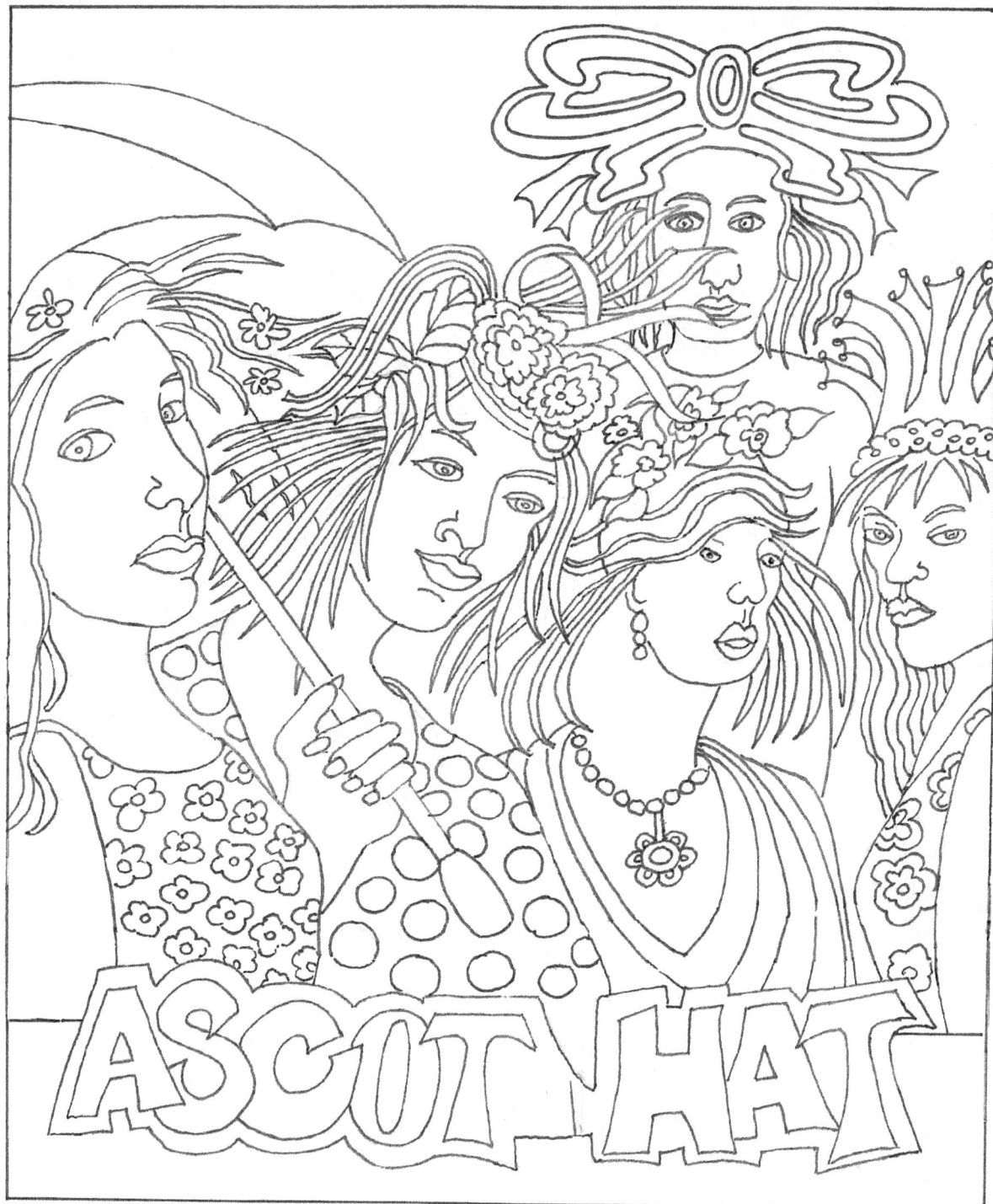

ASCOT HAT

Fashion

Your thoughts + notes

Your drawings + ideas

Poster

Your drawings

Your thoughts + notes

Poster

TARO

Book cover

Your drawings + ideas

ZODIAC EARTH SIGNS

Fashion

Book cover

Your thoughts + notes

Your drawings + ideas

Your thoughts + notes

Handout

pets

book cover

hobbies

Advert

FOOD·COM

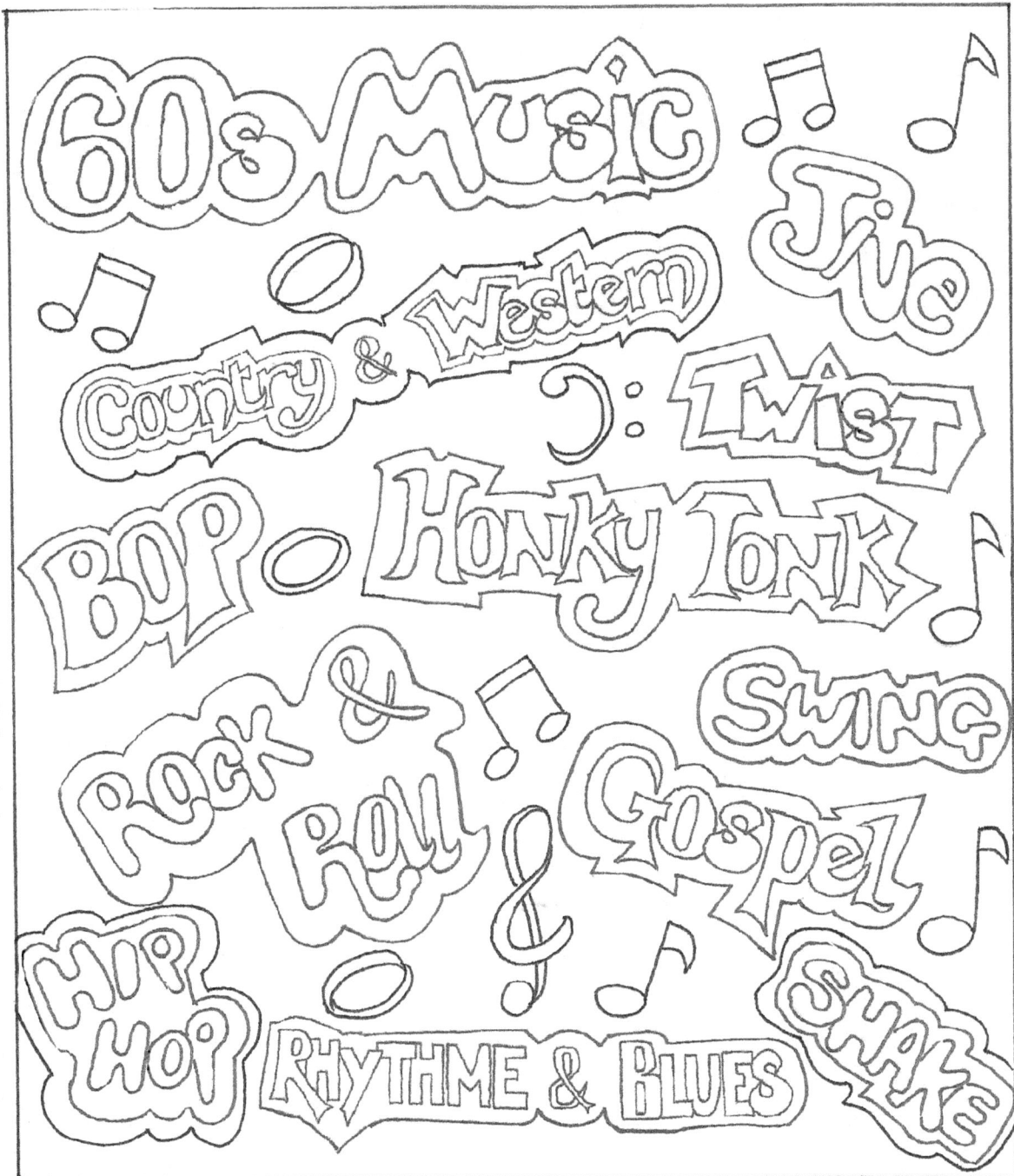

Poster

60s Music

memories

drawings

Your poems + songs

Fashion

Advert

Your thoughts + notes

COCKTAILS

MIX it

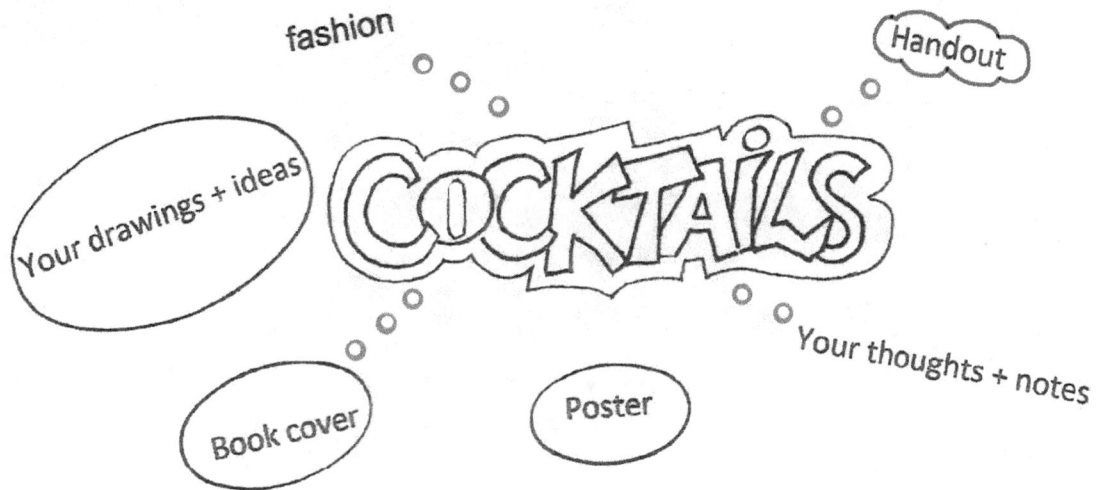

fashion

Handout

Your drawings + ideas

COCKTAILS

Your thoughts + notes

Book cover

Poster

ZODIAC

Advert

ZODIAC

FIRE SIGNS

ideas

Your poems + songs

Fashion

drawings + ideas

Fashion

Your thoughts + notes

Book cover

HAIR·IS·US

ZODIAC

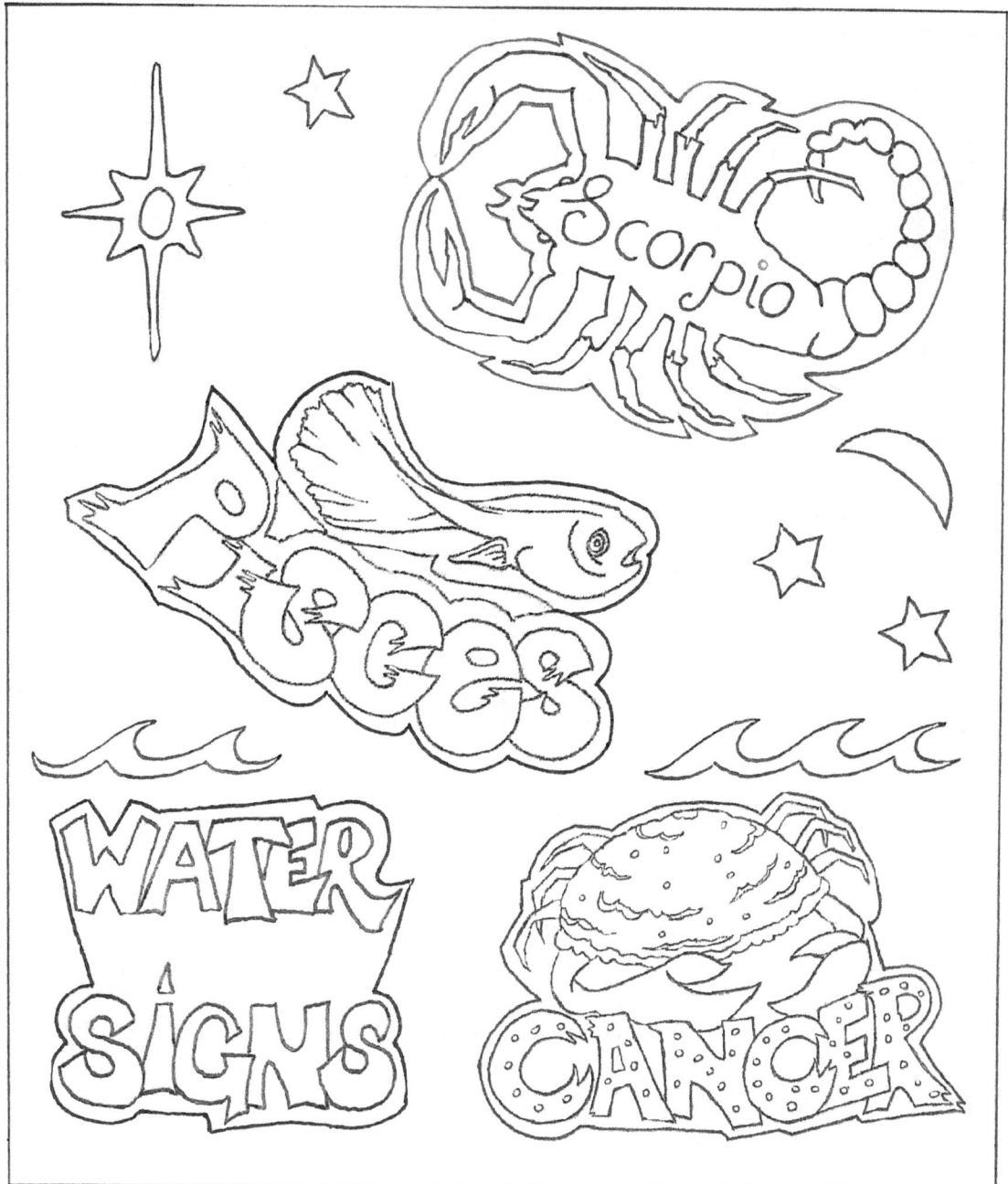

drawings + ideas °° ° ZODIAC

WATER   poems + songs

Your thoughts + notes   SIGNS

Book cover

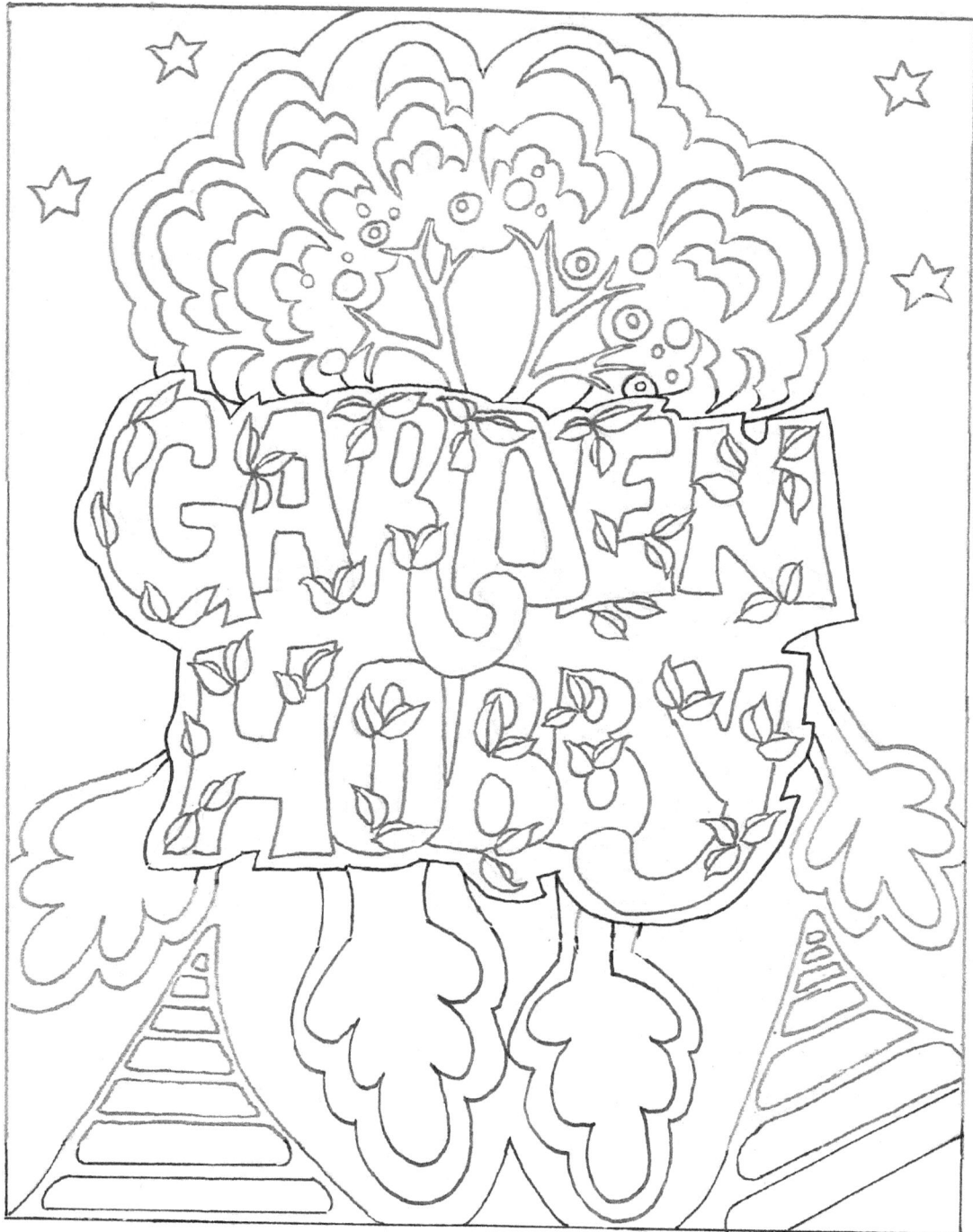

Your drawings + ideas

Fashion

thoughts + notes

Book cover

Hobbies

Your thoughts + notes

dreams

drawings + ideas

Friends

pets

Fashion

Your drawings + ideas

Let's

hobbies

memories

Your poems + songs

Sing

POWER YOUR CREATIVE BRAIN

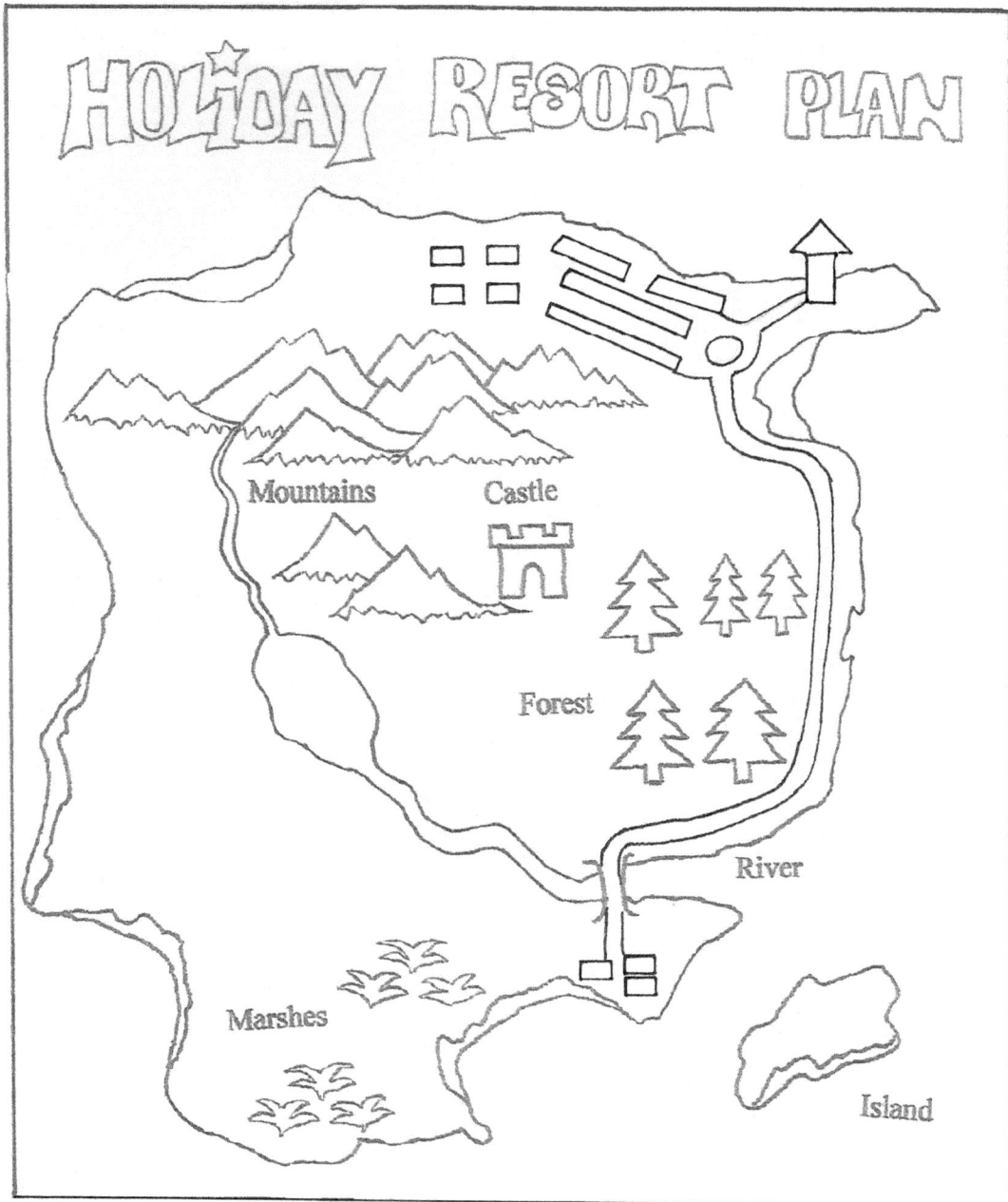

HOLIDAY RESORT PLAN

thoughts + notes

poster

Memories

Your drawings + ideas

www.ingramcontent.com/pod-product-compliance
Lightning Source LLC
Chambersburg PA
CBHW080525030426
42337CB00023B/4639